Cutting Edge Medical Technology

ReferencePoint Press®

San Diego, CA

Other books in the *Cutting Edge Technology* series

CUTTING EDGE
TECHNOLOGY

Cutting Edge Medical Technology

Toney Allman

ReferencePoint Press®

San Diego, CA

© 2017 ReferencePoint Press, Inc.
Printed in the United States

For more information, contact:
ReferencePoint Press, Inc.
PO Box 27779
San Diego, CA 92198
www.ReferencePointPress.com

LIBRARY OF CONGRESS CATALOGING-IN-PUBLICATION DATA

Names: Allman, Toney.
Title: Cutting edge medical technology / by Toney Allman.
Description: San Diego, CA : ReferencePoint Press, Inc., 2017. | Series: Cutting edge technology | Audience: Grade 9 to 12. | Includes bibliographical references and index.
Identifiers: LCCN 2016013792 (print) | LCCN 2016015959 (ebook) | ISBN 9781682820421 (hardback) | ISBN 9781682820438 (eBook)
Subjects: LCSH: Medical technology--Juvenile literature.
Classification: LCC R855.4 .A45 2017 (print) | LCC R855.4 (ebook) | DDC 610.285--dc23
LC record available at https://lccn.loc.gov/2016013792

Contents

Innovations in Medical Technology

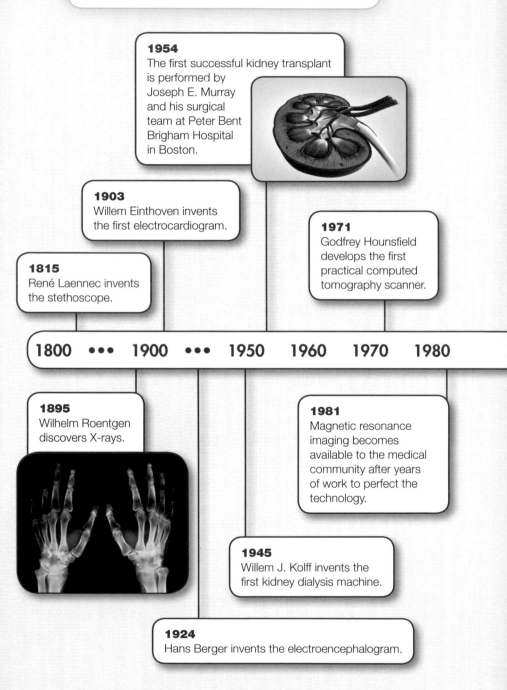

1954
The first successful kidney transplant is performed by Joseph E. Murray and his surgical team at Peter Bent Brigham Hospital in Boston.

1903
Willem Einthoven invents the first electrocardiogram.

1971
Godfrey Hounsfield develops the first practical computed tomography scanner.

1815
René Laennec invents the stethoscope.

1800 ••• 1900 ••• 1950 1960 1970 1980

1895
Wilhelm Roentgen discovers X-rays.

1981
Magnetic resonance imaging becomes available to the medical community after years of work to perfect the technology.

1945
Willem J. Kolff invents the first kidney dialysis machine.

1924
Hans Berger invents the electroencephalogram.

2006
Anthony Atala reports the first laboratory organs (bladders) grown from a patient's own cells and successfully implanted into pediatric patients with long-term functionality.

1990
Researchers begin the Human Genome Project funded by the US Department of Energy and the National Institutes of Health.

2015
The FDA approves a new kind of immunotherapy drug for treating advanced melanoma (a deadly skin cancer); it works by genetically engineering a virus to kill cancer cells.

2014
ReWalk Robotics receives the first FDA approval for a medical exoskeleton to be used independently by people with paraplegia due to spinal cord injuries.

2002
The International HapMap Project begins, with the goal of identifying common gene variations in humans so as to discover the genes affecting health and disease.

1990   **2000**   **2010**

2000
The da Vinci Surgical System becomes the first robotic surgical system to receive US Food and Drug Administration (FDA) approval.

2009
Apple demonstrates how health devices such as blood pressure monitors and blood glucose meters can connect to a smartphone.

2003
Mapping of the human genome is completed.

2008
The 1000 Genomes Project begins with the goal of sequencing the whole genomes of twenty-five hundred individuals.

Into the Future

In the fictional *Star Trek* world, Dr. Leonard McCoy uses a hand-held tricorder to perform a medical examination without ever touching the patient. In September 2016 dozens of consumer volunteers began testing just such devices to determine whether an actual, working tricorder could become a reality. The volunteers evaluated their bodies for overall health and the presence of medical problems with tricorder-like tools developed by seven different research teams as part of a worldwide competition. The competition is sponsored by the nonprofit XPRIZE foundation. In 2012, with the sponsorship of the telecommunications company Qualcomm, the Qualcomm Tricorder XPRIZE competition began, with awards worth $10 million. The winners of the contest will be decided in 2017.

How to Build a Good Tricorder

The rules of the competition are daunting. Each competing research team must develop a handheld digital device weighing no more than 5 pounds (2.3 kg). The tricorder must be able to read basic vital signs, such as blood pressure, heart rate, respiratory rate, and temperature. In addition, it has to accurately diagnose twelve disease conditions: anemia, urinary tract infection, diabetes, atrial fibrillation, stroke, sleep apnea, tuberculosis, chronic obstructive pulmonary disease, pneumonia, otitis (ear infection), leukocytosis (a high white blood cell count), and hepatitis. It also must be able to determine that a person does not have any of these problems.

Three hundred teams entered the contest in 2012, but by 2013 just thirty-four were still trying for the prize. In 2014 the ten best teams were chosen on the basis of the success of their designs, and those teams were then challenged to finalize their devices, build and submit thirty units, and add three more diseases, such as whooping cough, to their diagnostic repertoire. As of 2016 seven finalists were in contention. The ultimate goal of the XPRIZE competition is to bring quality health care and diagnosis to individuals. The finalists will be judged by that standard, including ease of use for regular people. The website for the Qualcomm Tricorder XPRIZE says, "The winner will be the team with the technology that most accurately diagnoses a set of diseases independent of a healthcare professional or facility, and that provides the best consumer user experience with its device."[1]

Toward That Final Frontier

One of the finalist teams competing for the prize is led by emergency medicine physician Basil Harris. Harris was an engineer before he became a medical doctor. His father and a brother are engineers. Another brother is an expert in computer science. Harris was fascinated by the competition to build a tricorder, and he got his family to help him. He says, "We were a bunch of geeks in that house. This kind of thing was in our blood. The idea of trying to bring this icon to life . . . it was intriguing."[2] The device that Harris's team developed is a lightweight kit that interfaces with an iPad. It uses sensors to assess vital signs, includes an easy urine sample test, and also asks health questions to which the patient inputs answers. In one way, the device that wins the competition will be even better than a tricorder. In *Star Trek* the tricorder scanned the patient, but the McCoy character made the diagnosis. The entries for the Qualcomm Tricorder XPRIZE must make the diagnosis, independent of a doctor. Harris says, "They made it much harder because now the decision is in the hands of the device. The machine has to collect the information and automatically make a diagnosis. It's a much bigger challenge than on the TV show."[3]

atrial fibrillation

An irregular and fast heartbeat that causes symptoms such as fatigue and shortness of breath.

No one expects that devices like tricorders will ever replace physicians and medical staff, but Harris does think that technology

Inspired by the handheld tricorder (pictured) of Star Trek *fame, the nonprofit XPRIZE foundation has offered $10 million in awards to international research teams who create similar devices that can be used to diagnose various medical conditions.*

can improve health care and help people make better decisions about their health. He imagines a time when tricorder-like devices will help physicians deliver better and more accurate care. He knows that tricorders will not be available anytime soon, but he says, "My dream of the future, years down the line, is to have patients coming in with all kinds of devices like this."[4] Tricorders in the hands of individuals would identify medical problems early and let patients know when they should see a doctor. The technology would also provide doctors with specific, detailed information that would make diagnosis and treatment easier and better than ever before.

Medicine and Technology Together

Saving lives and improving the quality of care is why doctors have embraced technology since the beginnings of science-based medicine in the 1800s. The new technology of that time, including the thermometer and the stethoscope, helped doctors measure and diagnose medical problems. These tools were breakthroughs because they enabled physicians to evaluate what was happening inside the body. Then in 1895, physicist Wilhelm Roentgen discovered X-rays. X-ray machines allowed doctors to see dense objects, such as bones and tumors, inside the body and without surgery; they became critical medical diagnostic tools. In fact, X-rays were the only diagnostic imaging technology until the 1970s, when technology such as computed tomography, positron emission tomography, and magnetic resonance imaging scans were developed and gave doctors detailed visual images of soft body structures and organs. Also developed during the twentieth century were technologies to assist in treatment, such as hearing aids, dialysis machines for damaged kidneys, ventilators for assisted breathing, and pacemakers for heart disease.

otitis

An inflammation or infection of the ear.

Today the goal of innovative medical technology is the same as it was in the past—to provide better health care, whether with a tool like a tricorder or with any cutting edge technological invention. Each new tool is designed to improve quality of life, treat diseases more effectively, or diagnose and even prevent diseases before they can do damage. Some technologies currently under development include sensors that assess anxiety and stress levels by measuring blood chemicals; 3D printers to develop artificial body parts like ears or livers; robots that can take over tedious chores, freeing hospital staffs to concentrate on patient care; and battery-powered germ killers implanted in the body after surgery. Some of these technologies are already being used in medical settings, while others are still being developed and tested. But many medical experts say that the future of medicine is now.

CHAPTER ONE

Robots

Since 1985, when the first robotic arm was used to place a needle in a patient's brain to retrieve a tissue sample, robotic technologies have been implemented in many medical areas. Although still not common, robots are functioning as amazingly delicate surgical tools, improving efficiency in hospitals, and performing medical roles with a speed and tirelessness that humans cannot achieve. Dr. Catherine Mohr is the director of medical research at Intuitive Surgical, which developed the robotic da Vinci Surgical System. She believes that robots will become essential technologies in the future. She explains, "Robotics can give us greater precision, lower trauma access, changes of scale (such as being able to work on microscopic scale), as well as navigation and imaging integration to provide a 'GPS' of the body and allow the surgeon to more accurately find and treat lesions. These are all exciting capabilities that could result in new therapies that we can only imagine right now."[5]

Robotic Surgery

Robot-assisted surgery is already a reality. In 2000 the da Vinci Surgical System became the first robotic surgical technology to be approved by the US Food and Drug Administration (FDA). The whole system was completely upgraded in 2009 and is now known as the da Vinci Si System. The system includes a console where the doctor sits and a cart with three slender surgical arms and one endoscope arm that enables the doctor to look inside the body. The surgeon controls all the arms from the console and views their movements with magnified 3D high-definition visualization. The surgical arms have detachable instruments for hands and perform procedures such as cutting, suturing, and clamping. From the console, the surgeon can rotate the instruments, control the amount of force applied, and precisely perform very delicate surgical procedures. Although not an autonomous robotic system (since the surgeon is always in complete control), the da Vinci is considered robotic because it is computer enhanced and its arms and instruments are capable of precise movements, flexibilities, and manipulations that are not possible for the surgeon. The da Vinci Si System is used for laparoscopic surgery, which is sometimes called "keyhole" surgery. This is minimally invasive surgery that requires only small incisions (about 1 to 2 cm) and makes for a less painful patient experience and shorter recovery times.

lesion

An area of damage, such as a wound, sore, ulcer, tumor, or other tissue injury.

Today more than three thousand hospitals around the world have da Vinci Systems, and more than 3 million patients have had a da Vinci procedure. The system can be used for prostate and bladder cancer surgery, hysterectomies, heart and lung procedures, and general surgeries such as hernia repairs. Learning to use the da Vinci System does take time for a surgeon, and the system is bulky and expensive, but many surgeons consider robotic surgery to be valuable technology. Dr. Pardeep Kumar of the Royal Marsden Hospital in London says:

> The natural instinct of a surgeon is to be hands on the patients, so sitting at a console staring at a screen controlling a robot does take some getting used to. But it is such an immersive experience that I've been able to carry out more operations, more quickly and successfully than I could have dreamed of. I just bumped into one of my patients being discharged three to four days after an operation using the robot, instead of the three to four weeks it would have taken in the past.[6]

Researchers are working to expand the uses of robotic surgery into areas such as tele-surgery. The idea is to enable a doctor to perform surgery remotely, even if the patient is thousands of miles away. So far such a system is not feasible, because the slight time delay between the surgeon's direction and the system's actions

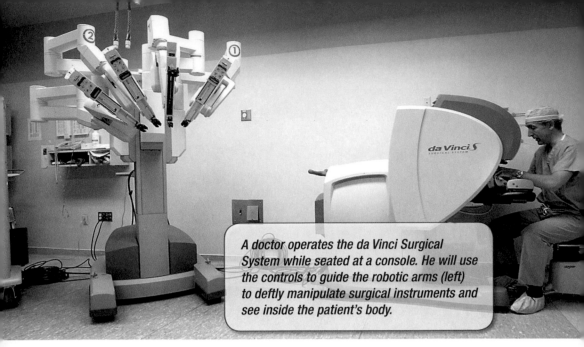

A doctor operates the da Vinci Surgical System while seated at a console. He will use the controls to guide the robotic arms (left) to deftly manipulate surgical instruments and see inside the patient's body.

could cause major problems and injure patients. The Raven Surgical Tele-Operation System is a research robot built by teams at the University of California–Santa Cruz and the University of Washington. Using the Raven, California scientists at the Center for Information Technology Research in the Interest of Society are trying to figure out ways to deal with the tele-surgery difficulties. They are experimenting with making the system more autonomous. The idea is to let a surgeon supervise the robotic action by inputting each of the steps of the surgery at his or her discretion, but then allowing the robot to carry out each step autonomously. In experiments with nonliving artificial models, the researchers have been able to direct the robot to suture and to make cuts appropriately, but there is still a long way to go before tele-surgeries become a reality. In the future, however, the researchers hope that partially autonomous robotic systems will be able to perform delicate, complicated surgeries—even on soft tissues like the brain—and bring expert surgical interventions to people anywhere in the world.

Medical Microrobots

In Israel in 2009 researchers at the Technion-Israel Institute of Technology, led by Professor Moshe Shoham, developed an entirely different kind of autonomous robot for medical use. Their invention was a microrobot only one millimeter in diameter and smaller than a mosquito. Named ViRob, this robot is built to crawl inside a human body. ViRob has tiny arms to push itself through blood vessels and—since it is too tiny to contain batteries—is powered by an external magnetic field. Shoham's team envisions ViRob as being able to clear blockages from blood vessels, deliver chemotherapy or radiation therapy directly to cancer cells in different organs, or carry a camera directly to the spinal canal to diagnose injuries. ViRob is not ready for human treatments yet. First the researchers have to develop a camera small enough to travel with the microrobot and also develop a safe way to steer it through the body without causing harm. The microrobot has been used in animal experiments successfully, but Shoham says that it will be a few years before ViRob can be tested in people. Dr. Sanjay Gupta, CNN's chief medical correspondent, says that ViRob "offers a glimpse of the future when it comes to medical technology."[7]

Many researchers see the field of microrobotics as the future of minimally invasive surgery. In 2015 an engineering team at the Massachusetts Institute of

> **autonomous**
>
> **Acting independently.**

Technology (MIT), for instance, built an origami robot made of sheets of liquid-soluble plastic. It is tiny and weighs just one-third of a gram, but it has a magnet on its back for power and can swim, walk, and carry a weight. The robot can fold itself up —for example, to make legs for walking—or roll around, and it will self-destruct by dissolving when its job is done. The MIT team hopes that someday the robot can be used for medical procedures. The patient would swallow the microrobot; it would be directed to its job site by the doctor controlling the magnetic field, and then when the robot had completed the procedure—perhaps delivering medicine—it would dissolve. Research leader Daniela Rus says, "You can imagine ingesting these robots and then controlling where they travel in the body. Once they arrive at the correct location they could form themselves into active instruments that can actually manipulate and help through the healing processes."[8]

Robotic Companion

Paro is a cute, cuddly, plush-furred, white baby seal, but it is not an ordinary stuffed animal. It is an interactive robot, developed by the Japanese company AIST for use with patients in hospitals and nursing homes. Paro coos and purrs when it is petted. Its eyes open and close and can follow movements around a room. It moves its head and limbs and can learn to respond to its name. Paro has sensors that respond to light, sound, touch, temperature, and motion. In many ways it is like a real, live animal, but without the needs of a living animal.

Paro's job is to comfort people with dementia or depression, who may or may not realize that the robot is not alive. Petting and interacting with Paro can help relieve loneliness, calm down distressed people, and make people happier. At the Livermore Veteran's Hospital in California, for instance, therapist Kathy Craig uses Paro to help confused and agitated patients feel better. Craig says, "We'll bring out the Paro robot and set it down and they'll start talking to the Paro, they'll talk to other people, it'll brighten their mood. And if they're maybe at risk of wandering and getting lost, instead of that happening, they might sit down with Paro for a while and spend some time with it." Paro helps therapists and other caregivers improve the quality of life for people under their care.

Quoted in Angela Johnston, "Robotic Seals Comfort Dementia Patients but Raise Ethical Concerns," KALW Public Radio, San Francisco, August 17, 2015. http://kalw.org.

Another robotics team at Johns Hopkins University in Baltimore is building soft microrobots shaped like starfish. The tiny robots are made with an absorbent material called a hydrogel combined with a biodegradable polymer (a chemical compound like plastic or rubber). The starfish arms swell and shrink so that they can grip things such as individual cells. The researchers envision these soft microrobots someday performing delicate surgical procedures such as biopsies inside the human body. Dr. Catherine Paddock describes the value of such soft, gripping microrobots, explaining, "The study is a good example of new robotic methods that help keep surgical interventions as minimally invasive as possible. The less that surrounding tissue is disturbed in sampling and removing tumors, the lower the risk of complications and the faster the patient recovers."[9]

Robotic Surgical Simulators

Quite different kinds of robots may help doctors train for complex surgical procedures or function to support medical staff and patients in hospitals. Some of these robots are already in service around the world, and others may be coming soon to hospitals everywhere. For example, just as aircraft pilots practice their skills in flight simulators, surgeons learning to use the da Vinci Surgical System need to practice the surgery before they use it on patients. The Robotic Surgical Simulator (RoSS) fulfills that need. It was developed in 2010 by Thenkurussi Kesavadas, a professor

Miniscule microrobots, depicted in a computer illustration, might one day travel through the blood vessels to clear blockages and repair cells. Researchers are already working on tiny robots of this type.

of mechanical and aerospace engineering of the State University of New York–Buffalo, and Dr. Khurshid A. Guru, director of the Center for Robotic Surgery at Roswell Park Cancer Institute in Buffalo. Guru explains, "Until RoSS, surgeons did not have sufficient opportunities outside of the operating room to gain extensive training in robotic techniques."[10] RoSS is built specifically to give surgeons experience with the da Vinci System and thus make robotic surgery safe, effective, and available for patients in many more operating rooms around the world.

John Vozenilek is chief medical officer at the Jump Trading Simulation & Education Center in Peoria, Illinois. It is a facility dedicated to research into medical education and simulation and has a complete operating room where robotic surgery simulators can be researched and tested. Vozenilek is enthusiastic about such systems as educational tools for medical students and all surgical preparation. He explains, "This is the way future surgeons will be trained."[11]

Hospital Robots

Remotely controlled robots are changing the way that doctors learn, perform surgery, and deliver treatment, but autonomous robots are on the verge of changing patient care in hospitals, too. One such robot is called the Aethon TUG. It is a trash barrel–sized robot that is designed to take on many everyday hospital chores, which would cut hospital costs, save time, and free hospital personnel for patient care. It can respond to calls or pages for pickups and deliveries from all hospital personnel. TUGs roll around the hospital on wheels and carry supplies, food, paperwork, and medicine. They deliver meals to patients. They also push linen carts and can tow 1,000 pounds (454 kg) of hospital equipment. In 2015 the University of California–San Francisco (UCSF) Medical Center acquired twenty-five TUGs. A laser map of the hospital and all possible routes was set up, and then the TUGs were programmed

biopsies

Surgical procedures to obtain small pieces of tissue from a living body in order to examine them for disease.

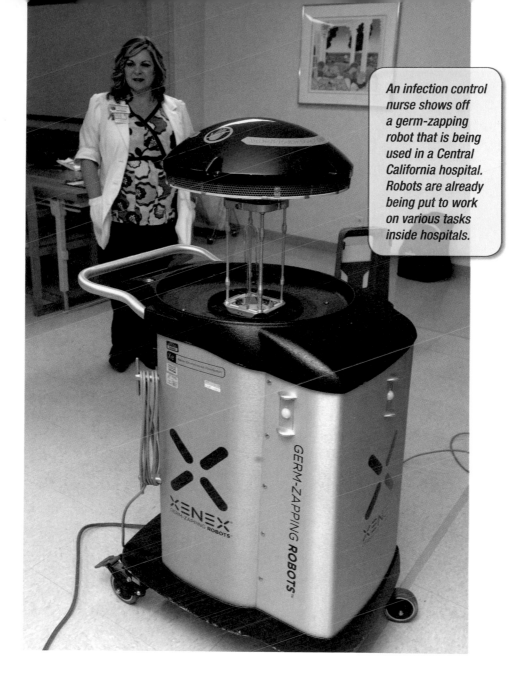

An infection control nurse shows off a germ-zapping robot that is being used in a Central California hospital. Robots are already being put to work on various tasks inside hospitals.

with this map. Using their arrays of sensors, the robots travel along hospital corridors. They go along different floors of the hospital, up and down elevators, and through automatic doors, avoiding obstacles and beeping softly to alert people when they are on the move. Brian Herriot, director of operations planning at the hospital, says, "The hospital is set up almost as a virtual railroad. . . . If they encounter an obstacle along the way, that's when they use their various sensors, laser, sonar and infrared to navigate around those items and continue on their path."[12]

So far, only a few hospitals are using autonomous robots as support staff, and no one has as many TUGs as the UCSF Medical Center, but many hospital leaders think that the robots will be used more and more in the future. John Krolicki, vice president of facilities and support services at the University of Pittsburgh Medical Center, says that TUGs are of great benefit to hospitals. He explains, "They're really replacing work that the employees did not enjoy doing. That's why they've been so successful around the country."[13]

Tele-Presence Robots

Robots are also finding uses in home health care services—for example, with the elderly or with the disabled. To help these people remain in their own homes and still have access to good health services, a Swedish company called Giraff Technologies is developing a unique mobile robot that lives in the home with clients. It is called the GiraffPlus. *New York Times* writer and professor of geriatrics Louise Aronson describes GiraffPlus as "a robot that looks like a standing mirror cum [with] vacuum cleaner, monitors health metrics like blood pressure and has a screen for virtual doctor and family visits."[14] Along with the robot, GiraffPlus is a system that has a series of sensors installed around the person's house, as well as wearable sensors to monitor the person's status. With a computer screen at its head, the robot connects with the computer of a caregiver or family member. The Skype-like connection allows the client and the caregiver to see and communicate with each other. The caregiver or relative also can move the robot all around the person's home, and use remote control to make the robot follow the client to other rooms. In one video of the GiraffPlus in action that is posted on the Giraff Technologies website, a woman is having trouble getting her new coffeemaker to work. She goes to the kitchen to show her caregiver, and the robot follows her. The caregiver sees that the client

Disinfecting Robots

Disinfecting robots are helping hospitals all across the United States protect patients from hospital-acquired infections such as MRSA (a kind of staph bacterium that is resistant to antibiotics) or even the deadly Ebola virus. These robots can move around a hospital room, operating room, or intensive care unit and automatically and efficiently kill all the germs within minutes. Unlike humans, the robots never make a mistake or miss a spot that needs disinfecting, and hospital personnel are freed from the risk of exposing themselves to dangerous germs. Some disinfecting robots use a hydrogen peroxide vapor to clean, but most use very strong ultraviolet (UV) light. This UV light can damage people, but the UV robots can clean a room without human help. The same rays that hurt human cells can destroy the cells of germs and kill 99.9 percent of viruses and bacteria on surfaces and in the air in less than five minutes. No one is sure yet that disinfecting robots will be worth their high cost in terms of protecting patients from infections, but hospitals are gathering data and hope that infection rates will be significantly reduced in the future.

forgot to put the lid on the pot and is able to help the woman use her appliance successfully.

The sensors in a house fitted for GiraffPlus can record movement patterns even when the robot is not turned on and no virtual visitor is checking in. This information can be sent to a caregiver or family member's computer or phone. The data is especially important in case the person falls and regular movement patterns suddenly stop. Caregivers are alerted, can turn on the the robot to contact the client, and send help if it is needed. Wearable sensors give information about vital signs such as blood pressure. If necessary, the caregiver also could remind the client to eat breakfast or take medication, particularly if the sensors indicate a problem.

The GiraffPlus robot without the house sensors has been installed on a test basis in more than forty homes in Sweden and other parts of Europe, and the GiraffPlus systems with the added sensors have been tried in about fifteen homes. Clients who have tested the systems report that they like the robot. They enjoy the regular virtual visits with caregivers and family members. It makes them and their families feel safe and secure, and even though clients may be housebound, they can still feel connected with the rest of the world. The GiraffPlus is a simple robot without a programmed brain or any autonomy, but that makes it affordable in comparison to robots such as TUGs. The goal of Giraff Technologies is to make such systems available to a wide variety of elderly people who would otherwise have to go into nursing homes or suffer with loneliness and the risk of injuries or neglect. With the robot, just a few caregivers are able to virtually visit and care for a large number of clients in their homes. Giraff Technologies call the GiraffPlus a "tele-presence robot,"[15] but one of the company's clients thinks she has a better name. She calls it the "lifesaving robot."[16] Without it, she would be afraid to live alone. Someday soon, Giraff Technologies hopes to see the widespread use of tele-presence robots that keep elderly people living safely and independently at home. Whether with simple robots for the home or complex, autonomous robots for hospital and medical care, robotic technologies are likely to play a large role in the future of health care for people of all ages.

CHAPTER TWO

Exoskeletons

Mark Pollock of Northern Ireland lost his sight in 1998 at age twenty-two, but he did not let blindness get him down. He became an adventurer and an extreme sports athlete. He ran marathons, competed in triathlons, and even participated in a race to the South Pole. He was also a champion rower. Then in 2010, at age thirty-five, Pollock fell 25 feet (7.6 m) out of a large, open, second-story window and landed on a concrete patio. Pollock remembers, "I fractured my skull, broke my back and the damage to my spinal cord left me paralyzed from the waist down."[17]

Regaining Balance and Movement

Pollock spent sixteen months in hospital and rehabilitation facilities learning to cope with his new disability. Despite the horrible blow of being both blind and paralyzed, Pollock did not give up on life, and he never lost hope of walking again. In 2015 researchers at the University of California–Los Angeles (UCLA) helped Pollock realize his dream of standing and moving his legs once again, not just for the pleasure of walking but in an effort to rehabilitate nerves and muscles that did not function. Pollock had no movement and no sensation below the level of the injury to his spinal cord, but the UCLA researchers believed that they could offer treatment that would improve Pollock's situation. The researchers used a noninvasive neuroelectrical stimulation on Pollock's spinal cord combined with exercise training and robotic legs to get some muscle movement and enable Pollock to take steps. Within one week, Pollock had taken thousands of steps in his exoskeleton.

An exoskeleton for humans is a wearable shell or framework on the outside of a person's body in the form of a full or partial body suit. Typically containing battery-powered motors, it augments human function. In medicine, an exoskeleton can help a paralyzed or injured person move again. It provides strength and motion to assist a person with muscle weakness or partial paralysis in regaining movement and balance. What makes an exoskeleton robotic is its array of sensors that detect slight muscle movements and respond by initiating electrically powered full movement. The exo-suit that helped Pollock, for instance, was developed by a company named Ekso Bionics specifically for people who have suffered strokes, brain injury, or spinal cord damage. To use this exoskeleton, the person straps the leg framework to his or her own legs. The framework attaches around the waist with a rigid brace. The person goes from sitting to standing with the help of crutches, and when the suit senses a shift in weight as the person tries to take a step, it makes a full step in response.

The Ekso suit, however, does not take over stepping completely. The leader of Pollock's UCLA research team, V. Reggie Edgerton, explains, "If the robot does all the work, the subject becomes passive and the nervous system shuts down."[18] This is not the outcome the team wants to see. Rather, the suit's purpose is to help the user regain muscle use and perhaps to retrain nerves in the spinal cord. For instance, Edgerton's team used the data from the suit's sensors to discover that Pollock had learned to flex his left knee and raise that leg a little after training with the suit and the electrical stimulation. This meant that Pollock was helping the exoskeleton take steps. The suit's sensors are able to recognize this movement and provide only the assistance needed to complete the step instead of taking over. Pollock's efforts marked the first time that a completely paralyzed person regained enough muscle control to help work an exoskeleton and walk with its aid. It is not a cure, but the stepping activity has many benefits. Along with regaining some muscle movement, Pollock's muscle tone improved, his cardiovascular system strengthened as he got real exercise for the first time since his accident, and his spirits were raised by the ability to be upright and moving once again. Pollock says, "Stepping with the stimulation and having my heart rate increase, along with the awareness of my legs under me, was addictive. I wanted more."[19]

cardiovascular

Relating to the heart and blood vessels.

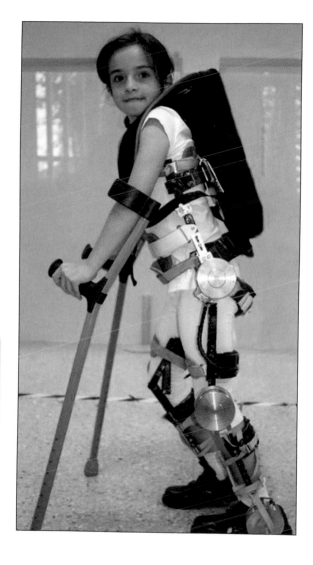

A six-year-old girl, disabled from birth, takes the first steps of her life with the help of a robotic exoskeleton. Such wearable devices can help create movement in people who have paralysis or muscle weakness.

Encouraged by Success

No one knows how well exoskeletons will work to restore motor function for Pollock or other people who are paraplegic, but both Pollock and the UCLA team are hopeful and encouraged by their success so far. Edgerton says, "It will be difficult to get people with complete paralysis to walk completely independently, but even if they don't accomplish that, the fact they can assist themselves in walking will greatly improve their overall health and quality of life."[20] If the Ekso suit helps the nervous system of spinal injury patients

From Theory to Application: Neuroplasticity

Neuroplasticity theory is the theory that the human central nervous system (CNS) is not fixed and unchanging but able to adapt and reorganize nerve pathways and function in response to environmental stimulation. If the theory is true—and there is significant evidence that it is—then recovering CNS awareness through repetitive movement should be possible, perhaps even after the most devastating brain and spinal cord injuries. This is the idea behind the use of exoskeletons to retrain the brain and spinal cord to regain nerve function and voluntary movement. Although no scientific studies so far have demonstrated complete recovery of CNS function in severe spinal cord injuries, studies have concluded that rehabilitation with exoskeletons can generate neuroplasticity. In 2015 one such study with ReWalk exoskeletons concluded that all study subjects showed great improvement in balance, and some participants showed improvement in nerve pathways, muscle movements, and muscle responses to electrical stimulation.

relearn or reestablish pathways for motor function by moving their legs through steps, it will be a huge treatment benefit.

As for Pollock, he continues to train with his exoskeleton, pushing himself toward further accomplishments. In January 2016 he wrote on his blog, "By day, I am a lab rat. I am shaved and willingly, joyfully caged in my robotic legs. I am wired to technology that unfolds the map of the inside of my body like the uncharted cosmos and with scientists, amateurs and other pioneers we explore it." All this experimentation has a big purpose and a worthwhile goal. He explained:

Then, as I walk in my robotic legs, the scientists hope that this weight bearing, this repetition of the walking pattern while my spinal cord is in this highly functional state will jolt it from its paralysis coma. Over time, we hope that this will develop the conditions to encourage my brain to regain some voluntary control over my legs. At that point the robot can power down and let my legs do some of the work. I understand it to be like the robot is performing the same role as a parent holding a baby's fingers and encouraging him to stand and to take some early practice steps before he even understands what he is trying to do.[21]

Exoskeletons to Retrain the Brain

Captain Trevor Greene, a veteran of Canada's military forces, is also using an exoskeleton to learn to walk again. He suffered brain injury during the war in Afghanistan when an ax-wielding attacker surprised his unit. The injury to the part of his brain that controls motor function left him unable to stand or walk. He also was unable to talk. He is the first person with brain injury (as opposed to spinal cord injury) to test the benefits of an exoskeleton. In 2009 Greene began working with a research team led by neuroscientist Ryan D'Arcy at Simon Fraser University (SFU) in British Columbia. D'Arcy believes that physical rehabilitation, even after debilitating brain injury, is possible because of the brain's neuroplasticity. In other words, with repetitive practice and training, the brain can organize new pathways to replace the nerves that were damaged. That development of new neural pathways is D'Arcy's goal for Greene.

neuroplasticity

The ability of the brain to reorganize itself and form new nerve connections.

By 2014 Greene had made some progress with his physical training, and he was able to talk again. The nonprofit Royal Canadian Legion raised $120,000 to buy an exoskeleton for Greene from ReWalk Robotics of Israel. The SFU researchers customized it to meet Greene's needs, and since then Greene and the team have worked to reestablish walking pathways in his brain. The work is not easy, but it is exhilarating for Greene. In 2015 he walked in public with his ReWalk exoskeleton and a walker and demonstrated his progress. He says, "It's like when you move

The Ekso suit (pictured) does not completely control a person's movements. Rather, it helps the wearer regain muscle use and possibly even retrain nerves in the spinal cord.

a doll's arms and legs. . . . That's what it feels like on my legs. To be doing that independent movement, even under power, is fabulous, because it's been nine years since I walked properly." He adds, "My hope is that it'll spark my muscle memory from the millions of footsteps that I took up till now."[22] That is the hope of the SFU researchers, too, and the hope of other brain-injured patients who are looking for recovery programs. Greene feels that he is helping those other people find hope through his own struggle. He is determined to walk on his own eventually. He knows that he has a long way to go, and there are no guarantees, but he says that someday he will hike to the Mount Everest Base Camp.

Future Systems

ReWalk and Ekso suits are just two of several exoskeletons being developed to get people upright, taking steps, and perhaps regaining motor function. These exoskeletons are not yet in common use. They are expensive—usually between $60,000 and $100,000—and they are bulky. So far, people cannot use them without professional assistance, and the suits themselves cannot perform all the necessary walking functions such as climbing stairs, pivoting, or maintaining good balance. Nevertheless, many researchers say that better exoskeletons will improve lives for people with spinal injuries—and possibly brain injuries—in the future. Volker Bartenbach of the Sensory-Motor Systems Lab of the Swiss Federal Institute of Technology is trying to develop exoskeletons with more flexibility, especially at the hips. He works for the day that exoskeletons replace wheelchairs for paralyzed people. He says:

degrees of freedom

In medicine, the various possible movement combinations through which a joint can move.

> Hopefully we will build systems that allow you to do more tasks. Besides walking in a straight line, you might be able to walk sideways in front of your kitchen counter or something like that, to walk stairs up and down. Also to turn round on the spot, so they need different joints, they need different degrees of freedom and if we had a system that was powerful enough to support you but also less constraining to allow you those movements you would be able to do such movements, even if you were a paraplegic or handicapped person.[23]

Researchers in Germany and South Korea are looking even further into the future and working to develop an exoskeleton controlled by thoughts instead of requiring muscle movement. With an electrode-covered cap that allows a brain-computer interface, one of the researchers has been able to make his exoskeleton take steps. He wears both the exoskeleton suit and the electrode covered-cap, which is able to detect and transmit brain signals activated by the eyes seeing flashing lights. On the suit, a flashing light is mounted on an attached arm on the front of the exoskeleton. When he wants to take a step, the researcher stares at the flashing light. His brain's electrical response to the light is picked up by the cap, which sends a signal to a computer. The computer then sends a step command to the exoskeleton. After a couple of seconds to process the information, the suit that the researcher is wearing takes a step forward. The whole process is clumsy and slow now, but in years to come, the technology may allow people with spinal injuries or debilitating neurological diseases like amyotrophic lateral sclerosis to move with mind-controlled exoskeletons that require no muscle movement at all.

Just a Little Extra Help

Other researchers are working to develop light, flexible exoskeletons that enhance rather than control movements. The researchers envision these partial exoskeletons as useful for senior citizens who want to remain active but no longer have the muscle strength and balance to do so. A research team at Aalborg University in Sweden is working on a robotic exoskeleton called AXO for this purpose. One of the AXO developers, Shaoping Bai, explains, "Many older people are mentally fit and want to continue to be active, but their physical abilities are steadily deteriorating. This is an attempt to complement the strengths of older people so they can continue to be mobile and live independently for a longer time."[24]

Bai and his team think of AXO more as a tool than a robot. With lightweight arms and legs, it fits on the body and has small electric motors that increase movement or strength by about 30 percent to 50 percent only, so that the person always feels in control. The

Helping Veterans

Exoskeletons today are so expensive that few individuals, rehab clinics, or hospitals can afford them. Recognizing the value of exoskeletons, nonprofit organizations supporting military veterans are raising funds to help. In 2016, for example, the group SoldierStrong raised the money to buy an Ekso exoskeleton for the Veterans Administration (VA) Eastern Colorado Health Care System so that it can be used for patient rehabilitation. The suit was the tenth exoskeleton purchased for veterans by SoldierStrong, which has the goal of donating eighty such suits to VA hospitals around the country. In 2013 paralyzed veteran Gary Linfoot became the first veteran to acquire an Ekso suit for personal use, thanks to the nonprofit organization Infinite Hero Foundation. In December 2015 the VA announced that it would begin to provide eligible veterans with ReWalk exoskeleton systems for home use, as well.

person using the tool is always stronger than the exoskeleton, but with its aid, such a person could go for walks, work in the garden, or even shop with ease. Bai says, "There are some very advanced and very costly exoskeletons developed for the medical world, but that's not what we're working on. The product we'll end up with will be more something you put on for half an hour or an hour if you need to perform a task that you can no longer do."[25]

The AXO research team expected the suit to be completely built sometime in 2016, and they predict that it will be ready to be sold commercially by 2020. They hope that the elderly will embrace the technology and be able to remain active with the assistance of a flexible, comfortable, and affordable AXO exoskeleton.

Physical Therapy and Exoskeletons

Functional lightweight, partial exoskeletons are already proving their value in physical therapy for the rehabilitation of shoulder injuries. In Madrid, Spain, a research team led by Cecilia Garcia

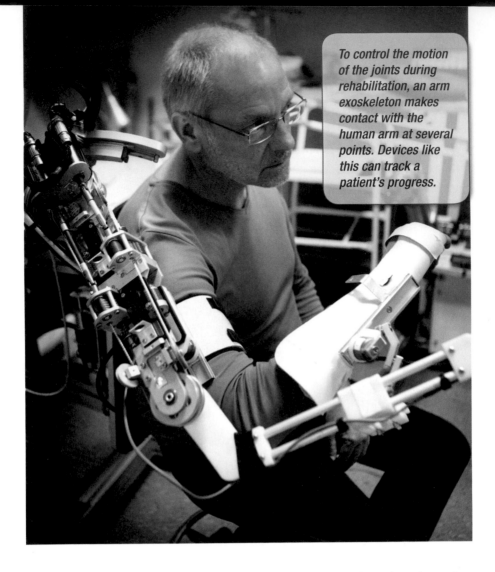

To control the motion of the joints during rehabilitation, an arm exoskeleton makes contact with the human arm at several points. Devices like this can track a patient's progress.

Cena at the Centre for Automation and Robotics developed a partial exoskeleton that fits over a patient's shoulder. The system can be fitted to different-size shoulders and arms. It assesses the severity of the injury and then moves the arm and shoulder in various exercises. It also records data on how well the therapy improves motion. It can be set to work the shoulder and arm minimally or more strongly as the patient progresses. Its use shortens recovery time for patients and also helps therapists. If a patient is being exercised by the exoskeleton, a therapist does not have to manually move the arm or shoulder for the patient. That means many patients could be treated simultaneously while the therapist just oversees their rehab exercises. Cena explains:

At the present, the physiotherapists do a hard work[out] every day with the patients, because they have to push and pull the upper limb during the rehabilitation session. Furthermore, they need to have evidence about the evolution of the patient. The exoskeleton can track all the movements and the data can [be saved] in the computer. The principal objective of our work is to give a powerful tool to the physiotherapists and help them to rehabilitate more patients at a time.[26]

Another physical therapy robotic exoskeleton is called HARMONY. It is a two-armed partial exoskeleton that wraps around the patient's shoulders and arms. It is designed for rehabilitation of people with upper-body disabilities that limit their arm and hand movements. As the person attempts to move, the exoskeleton enhances the motion, either as an assist (to strengthen the movement) or to guide the movements correctly. The system's array of sensors collects movement data from the patient at the rate of two thousand times per second so that the exoskeleton can immediately adjust its movement to the motion needs of the patient. HARMONY was developed by the ReNeu Robotics Lab in the Mechanical Engineering Department of the University of Texas–Austin. Its main function is to assist patients with serious neuromuscular injuries from strokes or spinal cord injuries in regaining upper body function. The system is similar to the exoskeletons designed for the lower body to help paralyzed people take steps. It is the hope of the developers that the exoskeleton will help people regain enough movement to be able to dress or feed themselves and perform other daily activities that are necessary for independence. The first HARMONY robotic system was completed in 2015. Its developers predict that it will be available for physical therapy use in about five years.

Many researchers believe that different kinds of exoskeletons are going to be common and valuable tools in the near future. Whether used to rehabilitate nerve and muscle damage or to allow injured people to function independently in the real world, they represent hope for people who previously had no option but to accept their condition.

CHAPTER THREE

Precision Medicine

Traditionally, when a person is ill, treatment choices are based on what works best for the average patient. All people with strep throat, for example, are treated with standardized doses of antibiotics that kill strep bacteria. People with high cholesterol are given drugs called statins. This approach works fine much of the time, but not always. Statins do not help a large percentage of people, but the factors in the patient's body or behavior that make the standard treatment a failure are not completely understood. With a cancer diagnosis, the standard treatments are one or more of these: surgical removal of cancerous growths, chemotherapy, and radiation. For a long time, doctors had no other options if these standard treatments failed. Today, however, researchers using advanced technology are discovering that each cancer has its own genomic signature. Genomic signature refers to the changes in a gene or group of genes that may allow the cancer to develop. Understanding that all cancer cells are not the same is leading to a revolution in cancer diagnosis and treatment. Drugs are being developed that precisely target particular kinds of cancer cells instead of treating all cancer cells as if they are the same. Individualizing treatment for every cancer patient will require much more research and drug development before cancer is finally conquered, but researchers are excited about the potential. And cancer is not the only disease for which a treatment approach at the genetic level might be valuable. People who have infections, high cholesterol, and heart disease may also benefit from precise, individual treatment plans yet to be discovered.

On January 20, 2015, President Barack Obama announced the Precision Medicine Initiative (PMI), a large, federally funded research program with the aim of bringing precision medicine to the prevention and treatment of many diseases. The National Institutes of Health (NIH) explains what precision medicine is and why it is important. The NIH says, "Precision medicine is an emerging approach for disease treatment and prevention that takes into account individual variability in genes, environment, and lifestyle for each person. While some advances in precision medicine have been made, the practice is not currently in use for most diseases."[27] The NIH believes that research in this area can pave the way to a new era of medicine that will provide individualized health care to prolong life and treat diseases more effectively in the future.

How Precision Medicine Works

Initially, with $130 million proposed for 2016, the PMI aims to collect research data from at least 1 million US participants. These volunteers are to be from ethnically diverse backgrounds and will represent different ages, genders, socioeconomic status, geographical locations, and health status. They would share their health records, answer surveys about their environment and living habits, undergo medical exams, and provide blood and genetic samples. All the

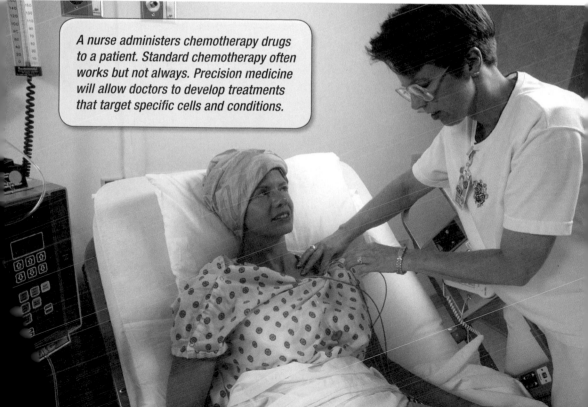

A nurse administers chemotherapy drugs to a patient. Standard chemotherapy often works but not always. Precision medicine will allow doctors to develop treatments that target specific cells and conditions.

data collected is to be made available to researchers around the country who will be trying to develop effective and successful precision medicine approaches to many common medical conditions and diseases. These could include heart disease, diabetes, obesity, Alzheimer's disease, and depression.

human genome

The complete set of a person's genetic information, consisting of all the DNA, including all the genes.

The PMI also allocates $70 million to the National Cancer Institute to help expand precision medicine cancer research in this important area, make personalized treatments available to everyone, and extend the science of precision medicine to more types of cancer. Cancer treatment is the focus of the short-term goal of the PMI because it is so promising. The science and the resulting breakthroughs are made possible by the modern technology available to medicine today. Dr. Francis S. Collins, director of the NIH, and Dr. Harold Varmus, former director of the National Cancer Institute, explain:

> The concept of precision medicine—prevention and treatment strategies that take individual variability into account—is not new; blood typing, for instance, has been used to guide blood transfusions for more than a century. But the prospect of applying this concept broadly has been dramatically improved by the recent development of large-scale biologic databases (such as the human genome sequence), powerful methods for characterizing patients . . . and computational tools for analyzing large sets of data. . . . Oncology [the study of cancer] is the clear choice for enhancing the near-term impact of precision medicine.[28]

Precision medical research is possible today because of the technological advances that enable scientists to map and analyze each person's individual genome—the complete deoxyribonucleic acid (DNA) content of the cells. Genes are the portions of the DNA molecule that form the units of inheritance that determine the characteristics and traits of an organism. Sequencing technology

Precision Medicine Ethics

The Precision Medicine Initiative raises some questions about the ethics of obtaining detailed information about 1 million individuals. Recognizing the importance of protecting participants' privacy, the NIH created a review board, which will oversee the project and ensure that individual medical records and genomes are kept private and not misused. The chair of the review board will be bioethicist Nancy Kass of Johns Hopkins University. She says, "It is essential that we get the ethics side of precision medicine right, too." Identifying information will be scrubbed from the medical databases, and every effort will be made to release personal data only to the individual who submitted it. Nevertheless, some critics worry about the government's plan to store such a large amount of data. Some fear that the computers will be vulnerable to hacking and that, with enough data, medical information could be traced back to specific people or families. Others worry that someday health insurance providers might use information about genetic disease risks to discriminate against people. Even with the best intentions, privacy could be violated. Finally, some people worry that volunteers will not understand completely what they are getting into; this is an issue of informed consent. The NIH promises to protect study participants responsibly and to make privacy issues a major ongoing concern of the initiative.

Quoted in Leah Ramsay, "Hopkins Bioethicist Nancy Kass to Chair Board Overseeing Historic NIH Study," Hub, March 8, 2016. http://hub.jhu.edu.

systems for individual human genomes are now available at a cost of just a few thousand dollars. The first human genome sequence cost about $3 billion. Supercomputers of today can sequence eighteen thousand genomes a year. It took thirteen years to sequence the first human genome, which was finished in 2003. Now, in a timely and low-cost manner, scientists and medical researchers can begin to identify specific genes and individual variations in genes that may be leading to disease. And that ability is beginning to lead to precise medical treatments for some cancers.

Immunotherapy Precision Medicine

Emily Whitehead's story graphically illustrates the value of precision medicine in cancer treatment. On May 28, 2010, five-year-old Emily was diagnosed with the most common form of childhood leukemia, which is known as acute lymphoblastic leukemia (ALL). ALL is a cancer of the blood and bone marrow. In the bone marrow are stem cells that are able to mature into different kinds of blood cells. Some become red blood cells that carry oxygen to the body; some become platelets for blood clotting; and some become white blood cells. White blood cells fight infections. B cells are white blood cells that make antibodies to mark foreign invaders for attack. T cells help B cells and search out and destroy infecting agents. Natural killer white blood cells search out and destroy cancer cells and viruses. In ALL, due to errors that develop in the DNA coding, the bone marrow rapidly makes many immature white blood cells (lymphoblasts) instead of mature ones. These cells do not act like normal white blood cells. They multiply out of control—the definition of cancer cells—and they do not leave enough room for red blood cells, platelets, or normal white blood cells. They do not fight infections normally either. Children with ALL develop anemia, bleed easily, and are susceptible to infections.

stem cells

The body's master cells that have the ability to specialize and grow into a variety of the more than two hundred kinds of body cells.

Without treatment, patients with ALL will die. However, 85 percent of children with ALL can be cured within two years with chemotherapy to kill the cancer cells. Chemotherapy targets fast-growing cells like cancer cells. Emily was treated with standard chemotherapy, and at first it seemed to be working. The cancer cells in her body died. Then in 2011, when Emily was seven years old, she relapsed, meaning the leukemia returned. Her doctors tried another round of stronger chemotherapy, but in four months, the child relapsed again. Emily was one of the 15 percent of children for whom the standard treatment did not work. She needed precision medicine that either tackled her particular kind of cancer cells or

A medical student receives training in preparing a blood transfusion. Before blood is given to any patient, tests are run to determine the individual's blood type. This is a simple example of precision medicine.

altered her own faulty immune cells on a genetic level. She got that treatment from doctors at the Children's Hospital of Philadelphia.

In April 2012 Emily was enrolled in a clinical trial to test a new cutting edge type of cancer treatment developed by Dr. David Porter and a medical team at the University of Pennsylvania. It had never been tried with a child before, but Emily was dying. She had the kind of ALL that affects B cells. Her T cells did not recognize the leukemia cells as cancer and so did not attack and kill them. Emily's doctors in the clinical trial used a technique called gene editing to change that. Gene editing is a kind of immunotherapy, so called because it uses the person's own immune system (in Emily's case, the T cells) to fight the cancer. The doctors extracted T cells from Emily's bloodstream, taught them to recognize the cancer cells, and then put the altered T cells back into Emily's bloodstream to fight the cancerous B cells. Porter explains:

> We take their T-cells from their bloodstream. [Then] they're taken to a laboratory, where they're infected with a virus that carries new genetic material to the immune cell. An

analogy that I sometimes use is that the leukemia cell has a piece of Velcro on it. But the T-cell does not, so the T-cell, the immune cell, can't stick to it. What we are doing is we are genetically changing that immune cell to put in a piece of Velcro on the outside surface so now when it sees the leukemia cell, they can stick together. I think if you asked people back in 2000 and 2002, some of this would have sounded a bit like science fiction.[29]

Changing the genetic information in Emily's T cells worked re- markably well because sticking to the cancer cell allowed the T cell to attack and kill it. At first, Emily got very sick as the T cells went to work attacking the cancer, but three weeks after receiving the treatment, her cancer was in remission. Regular checks of her bone marrow in the months that followed continued to show no signs of leukemia. As of 2016, Emily was still a normal, healthy girl. The ALL treatment that Emily received is still available only in clinical trials, but fifty- nine child and young adult patients have received it so far. Ninety-four percent of them (fifty-five patients) had a complete cancer remission, but the cancer came back in 36 percent (twenty patients). Doctors determined that the cancer had grown in a kind of white blood cell that the T cells had not been taught to recognize. In these types of ALL, further precision treat- ment breakthroughs will be needed, but doctors at the Children's Hospital of Philadelphia are extremely encouraged by the thirty- four patients who remain in remission for at least a year. (As of 2016, one other patient had been in remission for less than a year.) The FDA has put the T cell therapy on a fast track for ap- proval for use in the general population for ALL leukemia.

gene editing

Treatment involving inserting, deleting, or replacing DNA in an organism's genome.

Individualized Lung Cancer Treatment

T cell therapy involves altering the genetic coding of immune sys- tem cells to attack cancer, but precision medicine can also be

The Basketball Great Saved with Precision Medicine

In 2008 retired professional basketball player Kareem Abdul-Jabbar was diagnosed with a form of leukemia known as chronic myeloid leukemia (CML). At one time, CML was a death sentence, but for Abdul-Jabbar and most other CML patients, that is no longer true. Although the disease cannot yet be cured, it can be managed with a targeted oral drug called Gleevec. Abdul-Jabbar's CML, like almost all cases of CML, is caused by a known genetic mutation. The mutation causes cells to accumulate an abnormal enzyme (a protein that acts as a catalyst for a specific chemical reaction) that leads to the rapid growth of leukemia cells. Gleevec blocks the enzyme and thus controls the multiplication of cancer cells. Abdul-Jabbar still takes the drug daily to manage his CML and has a long, healthy life ahead of him. He credits precision medicine with saving his life. When Barack Obama held a White House East Room event to introduce his Precision Medicine Initiative in January 2015, Abdul-Jabbar stood with him to offer support and to be a representative of the bright promise of precision medicine.

used to identify the parts of the cancer cell that cause it to grow and multiply and then target those parts. Corey Wood, for example, was diagnosed with stage IV lung cancer just after graduating from college in 2014. The twenty-two-year-old from Yorba Linda, California, had never smoked and was a seemingly healthy, active, athletic young woman. She was devastated by the diagnosis. Stage IV lung cancer is cancer that has spread, or metastasized, to other organs of the body. It generally has a survival rate of just 16 percent. Wood's oncologist, Timothy E. Byun of St. Joseph Hospital in Orange, California, felt sure that her particular cancer must be due to a genetic mutation, since she was so young and had no risk factors for lung cancer. He asked for permission to surgically remove one of her cancerous nodes and have it genetically tested. Wood agreed; one small tumor was removed and sent to a medical laboratory for complete genomic testing. The results showed that her cancer was positive for a specific mutation of a gene called ROS1. ROS1 mutations (abnormal sequences in the DNA code) can lead to lung cancers like Wood's.

Identifying the precise genetic problem involved in Wood's cancer led to a treatment plan called targeted therapy. Targeted therapy drugs are designed to work on changes in the proteins of cells that have allowed them to become cancerous. The protein changes in Wood's lung cancer cells were caused by the ROS1 mutation, and a targeted therapy drug is available for this specific cancer. It is called crizotinib, and it interferes with the ability of Wood's type of lung cancer cells to divide, multiply, and repair themselves. Precision medicine with targeted therapy was the treatment of choice for Wood. She remembers, "It moved quickly then. I found out I was positive for *ROS1*, picked up my Xalkori (crizotinib) pills three days later and about three months later, the cancer was completely gone: clear lungs, clear lymph nodes and the bone metastases were healing."[30]

Although Wood is still healthy, she cannot yet be sure that she has beaten lung cancer. Nevertheless, she and her doctors are optimistic about her future and enthusiastic about the promise of targeted therapy. Wood says, "Comprehensive genomic profiling and precision medicine together create a personalized treatment approach that targets a patient's specific genetic cancer mutation. . . . I am happily, and proudly, NED, 'No Evidence of Disease.' Precision medicine has put my cancer on pause. It is the future of cancer treatment."[31]

A Precise Diagnosis

Precision medicine is also invaluable in areas other than cancer. It enabled David B. Goldstein to diagnose and treat a rare disease in a baby girl before it disabled or killed her. In this case sequencing

> **mutation**
>
> **A change in the DNA coding of a gene that may be inherited from parents or occur during a person's lifetime from environmental damage.**

A colorized chest X-ray reveals a cancerous tumor (red-orange) in the lung. Through genetic testing, doctors identified a mutation on a cancerous lymph node near a patient's lung and developed a targeted treatment plan for that patient.

of the baby's individual genome identified an unusual genetic mutation that no one had suspected. When the fifteen-month-old girl was first seen at Duke University Hospital in Durham, North Carolina, she was a medical mystery. She had arm weakness, vision problems, and excessive drooling. She could not hold her head up normally nor walk steadily. Doctors at first assumed that she had an autoimmune disorder—a disease in which the body's immune system mistakenly attacks its own tissues or organs. The assumption was logical since her symptoms were consistent with such a diagnosis. However, after four months of treatment for autoimmune problems, the baby showed no improvement.

At that point, she was referred to Goldstein, who used genomic sequencing to search for evidence of genetic disease. The testing revealed genetic mutations that are the cause of a rare neurological disease called Brown-Vialetto-Van Laere syndrome 2 (BVVLS2). The disease is progressively damaging and usually fatal if left untreated. It is also very difficult to diagnose before neurological damage is done. The genetic mutations cause a severe deficiency of the B vitamin riboflavin in the red blood cells, which causes all the neurological disabilities and damage. Once Goldstein had successfully diagnosed the baby, she was immediately started on high doses of riboflavin supplements. Within a month, the then twenty-month-old showed improvement. She stopped drooling and her motor strength increased. Her walking became steady, and she began to feel better and to play with toys. Most importantly, the progressive neurological damage was halted. The baby showed no worsening of any symptoms.

This baby was the youngest child ever to be correctly diagnosed with BVVLS2 and therefore the most successfully prevented from developing permanent disability. Goldstein says, "Being able to diagnose a genetic disease doesn't always mean we're able to use what we know to treat or cure the patient, so this case was unusual. Nonetheless, it demonstrates how . . . genome sequencing can benefit patients. As we learn more about the genetics of disease and discover new treatments, cases like this will become increasingly common."[32]

Toward Better Patient Care

Goldstein believes that genome sequencing should be used in all childhood diseases for which a genetic cause is suspected, because often the earlier treatment is begun, the better the outcome for the patient. Alexander Parker, associate director of the Mayo Clinic Center for Individualized Medicine, agrees with him. At the center, a young man named Dustin Bennett finally received a diagnosis for the genetic disorder that had plagued him all his life. Doctors were then able to treat him with the right medication to improve his neurological condition and make movement easier for him. Parker says, "Since the sequencing of the first human genome . . . we've been waiting for the technology to advance to a point where we can use it in the clinic to help patients. That day has arrived. Dustin is a wonderful example of exactly how genomic sequencing can be used in the clinic to find meaningful answers for patients."[33] When genome sequencing and treatments targeting diseases at the genetic level become a typical part of health care, the promise of precision medicine will fast become a reality.

Tissue and Organ Engineering

If only people could grow missing or damaged organs and tissues like a lizard can grow a new tail. If only 3D printers could make new tissues and organs for people that would function like the real things. This is the hope of tissue and organ engineering. It is a hope that may never be realized, but despite the difficulties, some medical researchers are trying to make the dream come true. Already, the progress is both startling and encouraging.

Anthony Atala's Vision

Dr. Anthony Atala is the director of the Institute for Regenerative Medicine at the Wake Forest School of Medicine in North Carolina. Atala says, "In theory, anything that is inside the body can be grown outside the body. The dream of regenerative medicine is to have fully functional, off-the-shelf organs and tissues to replace diseased or damaged organs in the body. We really hope that these technologies will be able to not only help improve lives in terms of quality but eventually also save lives."[34]

Since the late 1990s Atala and his teams of researchers have been trying to find ways to grow organs and tissues in the laboratory that can be transplanted into people who need them. They have succeeded in growing more than thirty different kinds of human tissue so far, but the technology is still not ready for general use. Regeneration is a complicated process, and getting FDA approval for new therapies is a slow, difficult procedure. Nevertheless, Atala and his team have achieved some remarkable successes, and they believe in a bright future for engineering new human organs.

A New Bladder for Luke

In 2001 Atala grew human bladders in his laboratory and transplanted them into seven children whose own bladders were damaged. Luke Massella was one of these children. Luke was born

with a condition called spina bifida, in which a part of the spinal cord is not completely enclosed in the protective spinal column, or backbone. Spina bifida can cause damage to the spinal cord and nerves, which may result in physical disabilities ranging from mild to severe. Usually, the physical and nerve damage occurs below the level of the spinal opening. As a result of spina bifida, Luke's bladder did not grow along with the rest of his body. As he grew bigger, his bladder leaked urine that backed up into his kidneys. By the time he was ten years old, his kidneys were failing, and toxins (or poisons) were building up in his blood. Luke became very ill. He was weak and tired all the time and lost 25 percent of his body weight. Without treatment, he would die. Atala asked Luke and his parents to consider an extraordinary new procedure: Atala would grow a new bladder for Luke to replace the failing one. The family agreed, and Atala got to work.

regenerative

Refers to the renewal or restoring of a body part.

First, Atala took out a small piece of Luke's bladder in order to retrieve some of its healthy cells. He put these cells in a petri dish with a special nutrient mixture that gave them food to grow, just as they would have inside a human body. The cells grew and divided until there were millions of them. Then, Atala built a scaffold—a mold—in the balloon shape of a bladder. He painted the bladder cells onto the scaffold, where the cells continued to grow into the right shape in an incubator until they became a whole new bladder. In about two months, the new bladder, made from Luke's own cells, was ready. Luke's old, nonfunctional bladder was cut open and surgically attached to the newly engineered one. (That way, doctors did not have to attach the new bladder to the tubes from the kidney, and the transplant was easier.) The procedure worked, and Luke grew healthy again. In most organ transplants, with organs from a donor or a deceased person, the body's immune system tries to reject the organ and attacks it as if it were a foreign invader. Patients have to take strong immune-suppressing drugs for life to prevent rejection. Luke had no such problems, because his new organ was grown from his own cells.

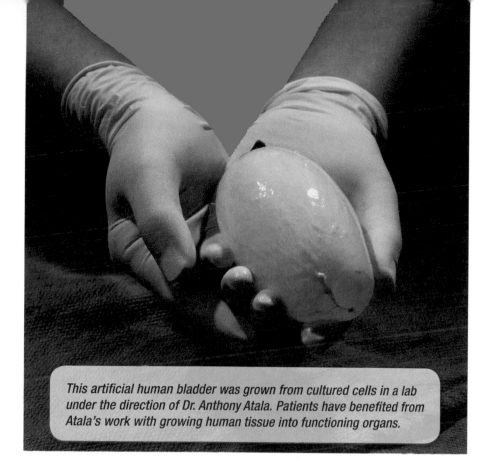

This artificial human bladder was grown from cultured cells in a lab under the direction of Dr. Anthony Atala. Patients have benefited from Atala's work with growing human tissue into functioning organs.

Today Luke Massella remains a healthy young man. He was on his high school wrestling team, he enrolled in college and graduated, and he went on to become a wrestling coach at a high school. All seven of the children who received the new bladders did well. One of the other patients, sixteen-year-old Kaitlyne McNamara, had to wear diapers before the surgery and was delighted to be able to be free of them afterward. In 2006 she rejoiced, "Now that I've had the transplant, my body actually does what I want it to do. Now I can go have fun and not worry about having an accident."[35]

Growing Urethras

Atala was gratified with the success in growing functioning bladders, but he keeps working to solve more problems and take the technology further. He says, "I'm happy when something works, but I don't really celebrate in the way you might think because there's always more work to do until we're actually done. We solve one challenge, and we move on to the next."[36] Atala and his team of researchers have taken on many challenges and have realized several more accomplishments in organ engineering. They have engineered urethras—the tubes or ducts that carry urine outside the body from bladders—in the same manner that they grew bladders. Atala explains, "Tubular, narrow structures are complex to build because they tend to collapse."[37] But the team figured out a way to build the urethras on a scaffold of muscle and other cells. With this method, the urethra and scaffold can be transplanted together into a patient. The scaffold then dissolves harmlessly in the body, leaving only the new urethra behind.

scaffold

A platform or structure that provides the needed form or shape for growing cells into organs.

Between 2004 and 2007, the team surgically transplanted urethras into five boys aged ten to fourteen whose urethras were damaged or defective. As many as 1 out of every 150 boys is born with a defective urethra. The usual treatment is to use skin grafts or repair the urethra with lining from the mouth, but these techniques fail about 50 percent of the time. The boys who received the lab-grown urethras fared better. The team followed the boys' status for at least six years and determined that the urethras continued to function appropriately. All the boys had less leaking of urine and fewer urinary tract infections, and they were more comfortable when they urinated than before the transplants.

More Organ Accomplishments

Using the same laboratory techniques they had developed for other organs and tissues, in 2014 the Wake Forest researchers reported to the medical world that they had successfully grown and transplanted vaginas in four teenaged girls. The girls had been born with a rare genetic defect in which the vagina and uterus are either underdeveloped or completely missing. After surgery to

From Theory to Application: Growing Partial Organs

One day Anthony Atala picked up a stone on the beach. It was shaped like a kidney, and running along the length of the rock was a ridge that reminded Atala of a similar line on a kidney, called Brodel's line. It is the line where the kidney has relatively few blood vessels in comparison to the rich supply of vessels on either side. Staring at the stone, Atala realized that he might not need to grow whole organs for transplantation. He could grow perhaps 10 percent of a kidney—a wafer that would fit right into the Brodel's line of a kidney in an easy surgical procedure with little blood loss. The wafer would be incorporated into the kidney and even though it restored only 10 percent of whole kidney function, that would be enough for the person to remain healthy and enjoy a normal life. Symptoms of illness do not appear until a kidney has lost more than 90 percent of its function. Today Atala says the major problems with turning his theory for partial transplants into reality seem to be solved.

transplant the vaginas, the young women were followed for up to eight years to be sure that the procedures were successful. In all four, the vaginas functioned normally, and the young women were able to be sexually active with no problems.

Atala and his team want to be able to grow penises in the laboratory, too, for men who have suffered devastating injuries, lost their organs to cancer, or were born with severe genital defects. Growing a solid organ such as a penis, however, is much more difficult than growing hollow organs like bladders and vaginas. Atala has been working on the problem for more than twenty years. In 2015 the team was able to report a successful penile transplant on laboratory rabbits. The researchers used many of the same techniques that they used to grow tubular and balloon structures, but they had to use a two-step process on a three-dimensional scaffold. The scientists collected two different kinds of cells from

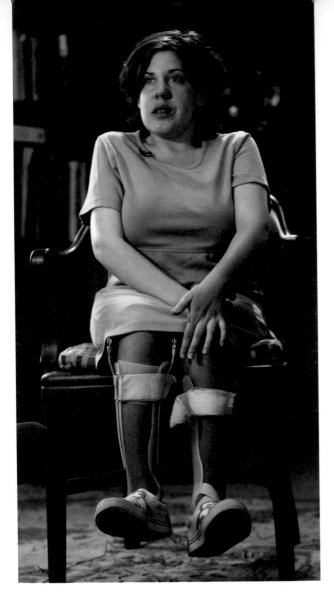

Kaitlyne McNamara is one of the patients who received a new bladder that was grown from human tissue in a lab. This is just one example of regenerative medicine.

the rabbits' penises—smooth muscle cells and endothelial cells (cells that line blood vessel walls and other spaces in the penis). Collecting the cells is almost always possible, even when a penis is missing. Atala explains, "The phallus [penis] is actually much longer than you think. It goes all the way behind the pelvis, so no matter the extent of the damage, there is a high probability that there are salvageable cells."[38] Both kinds of cells were injected onto the scaffold on separate days, and within one month, the cells multiplied and began organizing themselves into penile tissue with correct structures. When the engineered penises were transplanted onto the male rabbits, they seemed to function normally. The rabbits not only had normal sexual function, they were able to produce offspring.

This experiment represents the first time that a solid, lab-engineered, fully functional organ has been successfully transplanted. It is a wonderful advance in tissue engineering, but success with rabbits is a long way from success with humans. "Even though we can make them in a very small mammal, we have to tweak the technology, the processes, the ratio of cells and so on, to get larger and larger structures," explains Atala. The team hopes to try human penis transplantation within about five years. Atala says, "It's a rigorous testing schedule. But we're trying to get approval from the US Food and Drug Administration so we know everything is perfect before we move to a first in-man test."[39]

Printing a Kidney

Even as the research with penises continues, Atala's team is working on producing other solid organs engineered from a person's own cells. This work is being done with 3D printing technology. The theory is that organ engineering for complex organs can be done more reliably and precisely and with fewer errors using printer technology than with petri dishes in the laboratory. A major goal is to build a functioning kidney. More than 130,000 people are on waiting lists for organ donors and transplants, and more than 80 percent of those people are waiting for a kidney. On average, twenty people die every day because no suitable donor organ has become available. Atala says, "The ultimate goal of regenerative medicine—regardless of the way the organs are engineered—is to help solve the shortage of donor organs."[40] The researchers in Atala's laboratories developed a custom-designed 3D printer called the Integrative Tissue and Organ Printing System (ITOP). Instead of ink, the printer's cartridge holds cells. Instead

> **graft**
>
> A piece of skin, bone, or other tissue cut from one part of the body and transplanted to another part in order to repair damage.

The Military Sees Value in 3D Organs

Miniature organs that function like real organs are of great interest to the US military. In 2013 the Space and Naval Warfare Systems Center gave $24 million to the Institute for Regenerative Medicine to fund research into 3D printing of miniature organs. Someday such artificial and reliably and accurately constructed organs could help protect military personnel in dangerous situations. They may be used to test the effects on the human body of deadly diseases such as Ebola or of biological warfare chemicals such as ricin or sarin gas. Once the body's reactions are fully understood, then research into treatments or prevention techniques could begin. Anthony Atala explains, "Miniature lab-engineered organ-like hearts, lungs, livers, and blood vessels—linked together with a circulating blood substitute—will be used both to predict the effects of chemical and biologic agents and to test the effectiveness of potential treatments." Such research could never be carried out with live human subjects, but it would harm no one when done with laboratory-made miniature organs that are not part of a functioning living organism. Effective treatments for soldiers and others exposed to biological weapons are the ultimate goal for the government and military when it comes to 3D tissue engineering.

Quoted in Joe Bargmann, "Wake Forest University's 'Body on a Chip' Program Produces Functioning Miniature Heart Cells in a Lab," *Popular Mechanics*, April 14, 2015. www.popularmechanics.com.

of paper, the machine uses a scaffold that is shaped like a kidney and made of collagen (like the cartilage found in ears and noses). The printer slowly drips layers of cells onto the scaffold. Once the process is completed and the whole structure has incubated and grown, the millions of living cells begin to communicate with one another and function as an organ.

Atala and his colleagues have shown that the technology for growing a kidney is feasible, but the research is still in the experimental stage. Such organs have not yet been used in a person or even in an animal. Nevertheless, the ITOP has also successfully printed human-sized ears that were transplanted under the skin of mice, as well as muscle tissue and fragments of skull bone transplanted in rats. Experiments with 3D printing and its benefits are still ongoing.

Just a Little Bit Might Work

Atala knows that it may be twenty years before lab-printed kidneys can solve the organ donor shortages of today, but he has another research idea that does not require growing whole organs. The scientists of Atala's institute are working on growing miniature or partial organs or perhaps just a piece of healthy tissue that could be grafted onto a damaged organ to keep it functioning. Atala explains, "Usually, a patient doesn't present with any serious symptoms till whatever organ is involved has lost 90 percent of its function. If I can insert healthy tissue, equal to 10 or 20 percent of the size of the organ, I can keep that patient functioning and alive at a high quality of life."[41]

> **collagen**
>
> A fibrous protein that gives structure to cells and tissues; it is a major component of cartilage, ligaments, connective tissue, bone, and skin.

Already the team has tried this approach with wafers of kidney tissue transplanted in animals, and the animals have stayed alive for months. They have used human liver cells to grow a miniature liver about 1 inch (2.5 cm) in diameter. A partial liver would have to be much bigger to function in a human body, but at least the experiment shows that the scientists are moving in the right direction. Atala believes that someday, he and his research team will be able to grow muscles, bones, fingers, toes, and even limbs that will replace damaged and injured body parts and change the lives of the people who need them.

Are Lungs and Hearts Possible?

Atala is the most preeminent scientist in organ regeneration today, but he is not the only researcher working on developing artificial organs. In 2010 Thomas Petersen and a research team at

A kidney is transplanted from a living donor to a patient who lacks functioning kidneys. Researchers hope to one day use 3D printers to create functioning kidneys—a process that experts say is feasible.

MIT grew a new lung. The researchers used a lung from a dead rat as the mold. They washed out all the cells with detergents so that just a kind of skeleton of the lung was left. Then they used lung stem cells, which can regenerate new lung cells, and blood vessel cells to cover the mold. The team incubated the whole structure until the new lung was complete and then transplanted it into a living rat. The lung worked only for two hours, but the experiment proved that new, functioning lung tissue can be grown on old lung scaffolds.

Lungs are not the only major organs that researchers want to be able to regenerate and replace in patients someday. Doris Taylor is the director of regenerative medicine research at the Texas Heart Institute in Houston, Texas. Like Atala, she wants to be able to grow new organs for transplants that will not be rejected by the patient's immune system. Her focus is the human heart. In 2008 she successfully grew rat hearts using hearts from rats that had died and washing out all the cells so that only a heart scaffold was left. When she painted living heart cells on the scaffold, the heart tissue grew and actually pumped like a real heart, although only with about 2 percent of a normal heart's strength. Since that time, Taylor and her colleagues have been experimenting with mammal hearts and human hearts from patients who have died. The team washes the old cells out of the heart and experiments with reengineering the heart skeletons with living cells. With some of the hearts, they have been able to achieve pumping at 25 percent of normal heart strength. The work is slow and difficult, but Taylor is not giving up. She says, "I think it's eminently doable. I don't think it's simple."[42]

Nothing about organ engineering is simple, but the scientists doing the research are dedicated to the idea of regenerating tissues and organs for the benefit of millions of people. They believe that what looks merely possible today will become tomorrow's reality.

CHAPTER FIVE

Wearable Medical Technology

Twenty years in the future, health care for individuals will look much different than it does today. Sensor technology will make personalized health and medical care available on a widespread scale and reduce the need for frequent doctor's office visits and lab tests. This is the prediction of Dr. Eric Topol, a renowned cardiologist and digital medicine specialist who says, "A whole new day is coming."[43] Topol predicts health management systems will provide data to help people adjust and personalize their diets, exercise regimens, sleep patterns, and medical treatments. These systems will be something like the fitness trackers of today but optimized by high-tech sensors in the home or worn on the body. He imagines, for instance, a bathroom scale that not only keeps track of weight but also stress levels, heart rates, and the air quality in the house. Sensors on dinner plates could measure calorie intake and nutritional values of food. Sensors in the form of skin patches or clothes would be able to monitor blood glucose levels, blood pressure, hydration, or lung function. If an illness or other medical problem developed, sensors could alert the person of the need to contact a doctor. All of these possibilities may lie in the future, but the capabilities for wearable medical technology are here today. Topol explains, "We can do things like never before, in a high-def way we couldn't even conceive could happen. . . . The pace of innovation is going to continue to accelerate, providing an opportunity for improved health outcomes."[44]

Smart Clothing

Clothing embedded with medical-quality sensors for monitoring health is already being developed. Smart clothes, as they are called, are wearable technology particularly suited for athletes. The fabric for smart clothing is usually woven with yarn that has conductive metal material incorporated into it. The metal acts as the sensor throughout the fabric. Sensors are any devices that are sensitive to stimuli such as light, temperature, pressure, motion, and many other physical properties. The sensors pick up the electrical signals being monitored and use a small transmitter to send the data to a smartphone, computer, wristband, or smart watch, where it can be read by the user. Incorporating this technology into clothing has several advantages. Since most people wear clothing most of the time, health monitoring would be continuous. And because the sensors would be touching large swaths of skin, data would be much more accurate than from, for example, a wristband. The wrist is okay for tracking activity, although even there vigorous arm and hand movements can be misread as steps taken. But it is not the best place for monitoring the heart, respiration, or other vital signs.

glucose

The main sugar that the body makes from food; it is carried through the bloodstream to all the body's cells to provide them with energy.

Several companies are offering smart sports bras, T-shirts, and tank tops that can measure heart rates. The prices are high as yet, with average starting cost at about three hundred dollars, but the apparel is available to anyone who is ready to wear the latest technology. The products are stretchy, close-fitting underclothes that fit next to the skin but have no bulky wires, belts, or straps to interfere with motion. They use the body's perspiration to form the connection between the sensors and the skin. People can use these clothing items to monitor their workout levels while exercising at the gym, running, or doing other physical exercise. With the data from the smart clothes, they know if the workout is building endurance, strengthening their bodies, or even going too far and exercising too intensely for heart health.

One company called Athos has developed tight-fitting shorts that measure how well the wearer's muscles are working. The shorts are called EMG shorts. EMG is an abbreviation for electromyography, a way to measure the electrical signal sent from motor nerves to muscles to make them contract. Each leg of the EMG shorts has six EMG sensors and two heart-rate sensors that

Smart clothes, displayed at a 2014 computer show in Taiwan, use Bluetooth-enabled sensors to gauge the wearer's pulse, heartbeat, muscle stress, body fat, and more. Wearable technology such as this has many potential medical applications.

send data to a transmitter and then to an app on a smartphone. The app has a graphic of the wearer's body that lights up with either blue or red to show how hard each leg muscle is working. The sensors in the shorts show which muscles are working hard (and how hard they are working), as well as which muscles can work harder. This information can be used as a kind of road map for how to correctly train muscles. Jacqueline Detwiler, for example, suffered muscle injuries as a ballerina and views the EMG shorts as a way to overcome her problems. She says, "Wearing the shorts is like having a personal trainer with X-ray vision. Lean too far forward in a lunge and the opposite hamstring stops lighting up. Slack off during squats and your glutes never go full red.

I had to go to Olympic lengths to get my useless right hamstring out of the blue–green zone. But at least I could finally see the path toward fixing it."[45]

OMsignal, a Canadian company, offers the OM Smart Shirt with box (transmitter and battery) and app for precision workouts. With its woven sensors, the shirt measures heart rate, respirations, number of steps taken, calories burned, and how hard the muscles are working. So far, the company has a smart shirt for men only, but it is working on developing a line for women also. One technology commentator, Drew Prindle, writes about OM Smart Shirts, "Wrist-borne fitness trackers and smartwatches are so 2012. In the not-so-distant future, all the cool kids will be rocking smart textiles to track their activity."[46]

Smart Clothing with Medical Uses

Smart clothing is currently most useful for dedicated athletes, but the technology will have medical applications in the near future. In Israel, for example, a research team at the Hebrew University of Jerusalem has developed smart socks with dozens of pressure sensors in the fabric. SenseGO socks are designed to help people with diabetes avoid developing foot ulcers, or sores. Foot ulcers are a dangerous complication of diabetes caused by poor blood supply to the feet and nerve damage to the legs and feet. Sometimes the ulcers are so bad that foot amputation becomes necessary. Danny Bavli, the team's lead engineer, explains, "This is a significant medical problem that affects the lives of millions. We thought there must be a way to avoid these wounds

conductive

Having the property of allowing heat or electricity to pass through.

altogether."[47] SenseGO socks prevent the problem by detecting pressure changes in the feet. A tight-fitting shoe, for instance, might rub on the foot and create a wound; the socks sense this pressure and send a warning to the diabetic's smartphone so that the person can alleviate the pressure before it leads to an ulcer. Other researchers also are working on smart socks for diabetics,

Sensors Inside the Body

A new type of "wearable" sensor is helping solve a medical issue that has been around for a long time: people who forget to take their medications or who take them at the wrong times. Unlike sensors embedded in clothing, this sensor is "worn" inside the body. It works like this: A patient takes his or her usual pill—except that the pill is far from usual. It consists of the patient's medication and an ingestible sensor. The sensor, which is about the size of a grain of sand, is activated by digestive juices that come in contact with the pill when it is swallowed. At this point, a signal is transmitted to a wearable skin patch that sends the information to a phone app—confirming that the pill has been taken.

Two companies—Proteus Digital Health and Otsuka Pharmaceutical Company—partnered to develop the first medication plus sensor system that will solve the problems with taking medication as prescribed. The medication they are using is called Abilify, which is used to treat schizophrenia, bipolar disorder, and depression—all serious mental disorders. Abilify was approved by the FDA in 2002. The ingestible sensor and skin patch got FDA approval in 2012. Approval of the whole system was expected in 2016. George Savage, the chief medical officer of Proteus, believes that drugs with built-in sensors will help millions of people in the future. He explains that sensor systems will improve health care just by ensuring that people are taking medications correctly.

and although none are available yet for the general population, the scientists believe such prevention applications represent the benefits of smart clothing.

Different kinds of smart clothes could be useful for many medical issues. Smart pajamas, for example, could measure breathing in people with sleep apnea. Such patients can stop breathing many times during the night, and the pajamas could sense when breathing was interrupted and sound an alarm. Smart shirts could detect changes in heart function for people with heart disease and warn them if a problem arises. Smart caps might measure brain waves and detect impending problems for people with seizure disorders. Smart clothes could even pick up signs of stress such as sweating and send a message to the wearer to calm down or, if appropriate, to a family member or doctor. Wearable technology researchers see an unlimited potential for smart clothing. Someday it might be able to detect small physical changes that indicate a person has contracted a virus, predict an asthma attack, or analyze sweat or blood for other medical disorders. Mark Pedley is the founder of the British wearable technology company SmartLife. He says, "I call it *Star Trek* stuff, but *Star Trek* isn't so far away."[48]

Smart Skin Patches

Clothing is not the only kind of wearable technology. Sticky skin patches that incorporate sensor technology have been developed and have a variety of uses. A British medical device company named Nemaura Medical has developed a skin patch that can measure glucose levels in the blood without needles and finger pricks. People with diabetes have high blood sugar levels either because they do not produce enough insulin to control glucose levels or because their bodies do not use insulin effectively. Over time, high glucose levels damage many body systems and organs, so diabetics have to monitor blood sugar levels to ensure that their medications and diets are providing good control. A noninvasive way to test blood glucose is needed. Nemaura Medical's skin patch, called SugarBEAT, fulfills this need.

SugarBEAT is a daily disposable stick-on sensor patch. It can be stuck comfortably on the arm, leg, or abdomen and left in place all day. The sensor is Bluetooth enabled and communicates with the user's smartphone app. The patch system works by painlessly extracting a minute amount of the tissue fluid surrounding the cells just beneath the skin and drawing it into the sensor. Then, Dr. Faz Chowdhury, the CEO of Nemaura Medical, explains, "The device detects and records glucose levels within the patch up to four times per hour, and this data is continuously streamed to the

electromyography

A diagnostic test that measures the electrical activity of muscle cells.

mobile phone application. The Patch is less than 1mm thick and designed to conform to the body, and provide a convenient way to track blood sugar levels throughout the day."[49] SugarBEAT is not yet available to the general population, but Nemaura Medical is seeking approval for the device in Europe.

Another idea for using adhesive skin patches with sensors has been developed by the Seattle, Washington, company X2 Biosystems. The patch is a concussion sensor that monitors the force of head impacts for athletes playing sports such as football,

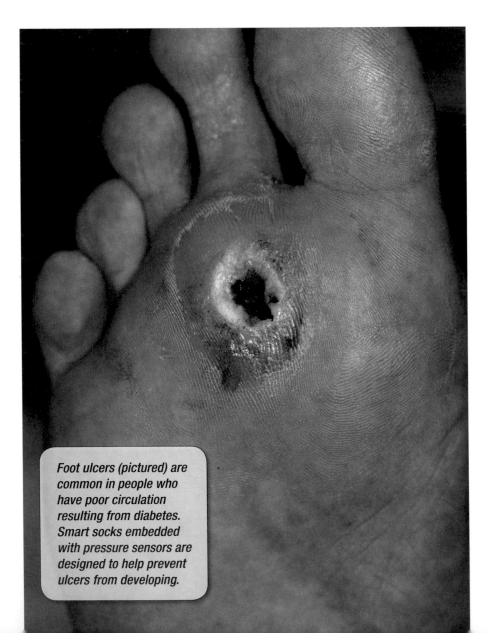

Foot ulcers (pictured) are common in people who have poor circulation resulting from diabetes. Smart socks embedded with pressure sensors are designed to help prevent ulcers from developing.

From Theory to Application: Bioelectronics

Bioelectronics is based on the idea that electrical devices such as sensors and circuits can communicate and interact with biological systems such as organs in the body. Behind this theory is the knowledge that most biological processes involve the transfer of electrons of atoms (having a negative electrical charge) and ions (charged atoms or groups of atoms) on a molecular level. Almost every cell in the body is controlled by electrical signals from the nervous system. The theory that electronic and biological systems can share information is sound, but in practical terms it is a challenge. Electrocardiograms, for example, represent one of the first uses of bioelectronics because they are machines that read the electrical signals of the heart. However, the heart is a large area of tissue with strong electrical signals. Sensors that read or communicate with small groups of nerve cells are harder to develop. They have to be miniaturized and precisely programmed in order to work accurately.

hockey, baseball, soccer, and rugby. The system has been used since 2012 by professional and collegiate athletes to monitor and reduce the dangers of traumatic head injuries. The patch is worn on the skin behind the ear, and it records and stores data on every head impact experienced by the wearer. The information is then sent to a computer or other device for analysis. The information helps medical personnel and coaches to understand what kinds of impacts at what strength cause damage to the brain and to develop playing and practicing techniques to prevent these injuries.

Gentag is a technology company that has developed several different kinds of medical skin patches with sensors that communicate with smartphones and computers. The patches are disposable, lightweight, comfortable, and no thicker than an ordinary bandage. The company has developed a fever monitor patch that can send temperature information from a patient to nursing staff without ever bothering the patient. It has also developed a skin patch that measures ultraviolet light exposure on the skin. With this patch, a person could avoid sunburn by receiving smartphone alerts that tell the patch wearer to reapply sunscreen.

Smart Bandages

Wearable technology is not only about monitoring and preventing problems. The technology might be useful someday for prevention and treatment in the form of smart bandages. Researchers at the University of California–Berkeley and the University of California–San Francisco have developed a stretchy bandage embedded with soft, flexible sensors that use tiny electrical currents to detect bedsores in patients. Bedsores are wounds that develop from prolonged pressure on an area of the body from being bedridden or immobile. They are the result of the blood supply being cut off to that area, and they can lead to deadly infections. Michel Maharbiz, the research team's head engineer, explains, "We set out to create a type of bandage that could detect bedsores as they are forming,

Researchers have developed a concussion sensor that monitors the force of head impacts for athletes who play in high-risk sports such as football. The sensor is embedded in a patch that is worn on the skin behind the ear.

before the damage reaches the surface of the skin."[50] Once they form, bedsores are extremely difficult to cure. So knowing early that they are developing can affect the success of treatment. Dr. Michael Harrison of the research team says, "This bandage could provide an easy early-warning system that would allow intervention before the injury is permanent. If you can detect bedsores early on, the solution is easy. Just take the pressure off."[51]

The smart bandage works because cells that are dying show different electrical signals than healthy cells. It has been shown to work accurately and consistently with laboratory animals. Maharbiz sees a great future for such smart bandages. He says, "As technology gets more and more miniaturized, and as we learn more and more about the responses the body has to disease and injury, we're able to build bandages that are very intelligent. You can imagine a future where the bandage you or a physician puts on could actually report a lot of interesting information that could be used to improve patient care."[52]

bioelectronics

The application of electronics to biology and medicine.

Many scientists imagine such a future. Researchers at Swinburne University of Technology in Australia, for instance, are developing a smart bandage made of a microfiber mesh that attracts and sucks bacteria out of a wound, thus stopping infections. Also, with the support of the National Science Foundation, a group of researchers from various universities in the United States have developed bandages that can be used for serious burns and other wounds. The research group calls these devices flexible bioelectronics. Flexible bioelectronics is the design and engineering of electronic devices, sensors, and circuits on flexible materials such as plastics, gels, and polymers for medical uses. The bandage devices are for delivering medication, monitoring healing by measuring oxygen levels and temperature, and communicating the status of the wound to physicians. Team member Reza Abdi of Harvard University explains:

> The goal is to have a smart band-aid system using flexible sensors and electronics. Current wound care or band-aid

technology is designed to protect the wound area from environmental assault. However, it is a simple technology, which does not provide any information about the state of the wound. Our goal is to embed sensors and electronics to band-aids which will enable (i) real time monitoring of the wound environment and in case of a need . . . (ii) intervene to remedy the external conditions (infection, etc.) by delivering drugs. We anticipate that such band-aids may be used on patients within five to ten years.[53]

Transforming Future Medicine

Flexible, wearable sensors represent the beginnings of a revolution in individualized health protection and well-being, as well as in vastly improved medical care. Such sensors could be used to monitor, diagnose, and treat infants with seizure disorders, athletes with training needs, people with chronic health problems, and hospital patients—among others. John Rogers, a physical chemist and materials scientist at the University of Illinois at Urbana–Champaign says, "The history of electronics is about getting closer to the individual. At first it was a computer down the hall, followed by a desktop, then a laptop, a phone in your pocket and a watch on your wrist. Now it could be electronics integrated [with] the skin, bioelectronics, and fully implantable devices."[54] The technology is just emerging, but the possibilities are endless. The sophistication of future wearable technologies is likely to change medicine forever.

Source Notes

Introduction: Into the Future

1. Qualcomm Tricorder XPRIZE, "Overview," 2016. http://tri corder.xprize.org.
2. Quoted in Eric Berger, "Emergency Physician in Finals for Qualcomm Tricorder XPRIZE," *Annals of Emergency Medicine*, January 2016, p. 15A. www.annemergmed.com.
3. Quoted in Berger, "Emergency Physician in Finals for Qualcomm Tricorder XPRIZE."
4. Quoted in Berger, "Emergency Physician in Finals for Qualcomm Tricorder XPRIZE."

Chapter One: Robots

5. Quoted in David McNamee, "Are Robots the Future of Surgery, or a Pricey Marketing Gimmick?," Medical News Today, August 1, 2014. www.medicalnewstoday.com.
6. Quoted in Mark Piesing, "Medical Robotics: Would You Trust a Robot with a Scalpel?," *Guardian* (Manchester), October 10, 2014. www.theguardian.com.
7. Sanjay Gupta, "Microbot on CNN," video. www.microbot medical.com.
8. Quoted in Melanie Gonick, "Robot Origami: Robot Self-Folds, Walks, and Completes Tasks," video, *MIT News*, June 12, 2015. http://news.mit.edu.
9. Catherine Paddock, "Soft Micro-Robots Could Do Biopsies, Deliver Drugs," Medical News Today, February 6, 2015. www .medicalnewstoday.com.
10. Quoted in Jacobs School of Medicine and Biomedical Sciences, "Simulator for Robotic Surgery Training," 2016. https:// medicine.buffalo.edu.
11. Quoted in Mike Koon, "Illinois Researchers Making Virtual Surgery Simulation a Reality," College of Engineering, University

of Illinois at Urbana-Champaign, October 6, 2015. http://engineering.illinois.edu.

12. Quoted in Althea Chang, "Pricy Robots 'Tug' Hospital Supplies," CNBC, April 30, 2015. www.cnbc.com.

13. Quoted in Alex Nixon, "Robinson-Based TUG Maker Aethon Builds on Health Care Trend," Trib Total Media, February 3, 2014. http://triblive.com.

14. Louise Aronson, "The Future of Robot Caregivers," *New York Times*, July 19, 2014. www.nytimes.com.

15. Giraff Technologies, "About Giraff." www.giraff.org.

16. Quoted in Giraff Technologies, "About Giraff."

Chapter Two: Exoskeletons

17. Quoted in Azadeh Ansari, "Blind and Paralyzed, an Adventurer Takes New Steps," CNN, October 9, 2015. www.cnn.com.

18. Quoted in Stuart Wolpert, "Completely Paralyzed Man Voluntarily Moves His Legs, UCLA Scientists Report," UCLA Newsroom, September 1, 2015. http://newsroom.ucla.edu.

19. Quoted in Wolpert, "Completely Paralyzed Man Voluntarily Moves His Legs, UCLA Scientists Report."

20. Quoted in Wolpert, "Completely Paralyzed Man Voluntarily Moves His Legs, UCLA Scientists Report."

21. Mark Pollock, "What the Polar Explorers Teach Us About Resilience," *Mark Pollock's Blog*, Mark Pollock Trust, January 2016. www.markpollocktrust.org.

22. Quoted in CBC News, "Exoskeleton Helps Capt. Trevor Greene Take First Steps After Axe Attack," September 17, 2015. www.cbc.ca.

23. Quoted in Jim Drury, "Exoskeleton Research Could Allow Paralyzed to Turn and Climb," Reuters, November 2, 2015. www.reuters.com.

24. Quoted in Aalborg University, "Exoskeleton to Ensure an Active Old Age," ScienceDaily, October 14, 2015. www.sciencedaily.com.

25. Quoted in Aalborg University, "Exoskeleton to Ensure an Active Old Age."
26. Quoted in Elizabeth Hofheinz, "Robotics Exoskeleton Aids Shoulder Rehabilitation," *Orthopedics This Week*, February 8, 2016. https://ryortho.com.

Chapter Three: Precision Medicine

27. National Institutes of Health, "About the Precision Medicine Initiative Cohort Program." www.nih.gov.
28. Francis S. Collins and Harold Varmus, "A New Initiative on Precision Medicine," *New England Journal of Medicine*, February 26, 2015. www.nejm.org.
29. Quoted in Linda Carroll, "Gene Editing Is Huge Leap Forward in Fight Against Cancer," NBC News, December 22, 2015. www.nbcnews.com.
30. Quoted in Andrew J. Roth, "A View from a Young Lung Cancer Survivor: Genomic Testing Provides Hope," *Cure*, September 25, 2015. www.curetoday.com.
31. Corey Wood, "Corey W.'s Story," American Lung Association, 2015. www.mylungcancersupport.org.
32. Quoted in Columbia University Medical Center, "Toddler's Rare Disease Identified and Treated Using Precision Medicine," ScienceDaily, October 22, 2015. www.sciencedaily.com.
33. Quoted in Mayo Clinic, "Precision Medicine in Action: Genomic Test Helps Solve Medical Mystery," ScienceDaily, February 3, 2015. www.sciencedaily.com.

Chapter Four: Tissue and Organ Engineering

34. Anthony Atala, "Regenerative Medicine 101," video, Institute for Regenerative Medicine, Wake Forest School of Medicine, December 2, 2015. www.wakehealth.edu.
35. Quoted in Carey Goldberg, "Doctors Grow Bladder Cells and Produce Rebuilt Organ: Milestone Work Helps 7 Patients," *Boston Globe*, April 4, 2006. www.boston.com.

36. Quoted in Steve Volk, "Engineering New Organs Using Our Own Living Cells," *Discover*, January 22, 2015. http://discov ermagazine.com.

37. Quoted in Amanda Chan, "Researchers Grow Urethra from Patient's Own Tissue," LiveScience, March 9, 2011. www .livescience.com.

38. Quoted in Dara Mohammadi, "The Lab-Grown Penis: Approaching a Medical Milestone," *Guardian* (Manchester), October 4, 2014. www.theguardian.com.

39. Quoted in Mohammadi, "The Lab-Grown Penis."

40. Anthony Atala, interview with Macrina Cooper-White, "How 3D Printing Could End the Deadly Shortage of Donor Organs," *Huffington Post*, March 2, 2015. www.huffingtonpost .com.

41. Quoted in Volk, "Engineering New Organs Using Our Own Living Cells."

42. Quoted in Brendan Maher, "Tissue Engineering: How to Build a Heart," *Nature*, July 3, 2013. www.nature.com.

Chapter Five: Wearable Medical Technology

43. Quoted in Rene Lynch, "Future of Health Care: Sensors Will Lead to Highly Personalized Care," *Los Angeles Times*, January 23, 2015. www.latimes.com.

44. Quoted in Tracy Cooley, "Dr. Eric Topol's Insights on Wearables, Smart Phones, Digital Medicine Revolution," BIOtech-NOW, June 17, 2015. www.biotech-now.org.

45. Jacqueline Detwiler, "These Shorts Know How Hard Your Muscles Are Working," *Popular Mechanics*, November 20, 2014. www.popularmechanics.com.

46. Drew Prindle, "One More Rep! This Shirt Keeps Tabs on Your Workout to Push You Even Further," Digital Trends, May 8, 2014. www.digitaltrends.com.

47. Quoted in NDTV, "'Smart' Socks to Help Prevent Diabetic Foot Ulcers," January 28, 2016. www.ndtv.com.

48. Quoted in Catherine de Lange, "Clothes with Hidden Sensors Act as an Always-On Doctor," *New Scientist*, April 2, 2014. www.newscientist.com.

49. Quoted in Ayliffe Brown, "Dr. Chowdhury Speaks About Nemaura Medical's Wearable Patch—WT Asia 2015," WT—Wearable Technologies, September 11, 2015. www.wearable-technologies.com.

50. Quoted in Sarah Yang, "'Smart Bandage' Detects Bedsores Before They Are Visible to Doctors," *Berkeley News*, March 17, 2015. http://news.berkeley.edu.

51. Quoted in Yang, "'Smart Bandage' Detects Bedsores Before They Are Visible to Doctors."

52. Quoted in Yang, "'Smart Bandage' Detects Bedsores Before They Are Visible to Doctors."

53. Quoted in Charlie Heck, "Not Just a Band-Aid: How 'Smart Bandages' Will Change Medicine," LiveScience, April 21, 2015. www.livescience.com.

54. Quoted in James Gerber, "Flexible Smart Sensors and the Future of Health," Engadget, September 21, 2015. www.engadget.com.

For Further Research

Books

Melissa Abramovitz, *Amazing Feats of Biological Engineering*. Edina, MN: Essential Library, 2014.

Nicola Barber, *Cloning and Genetic Engineering*. New York: Rosen, 2012.

Jennifer Kroll, *The Cutting Edge: Breakthroughs in Technology*. Huntington Beach, CA: Teacher Created Materials, 2013.

Elizabeth Lachner, ed., *Bioengineering*. New York: Britannica Educational, 2015.

Alexandra Morris, *Medical Research and Technology*. Edina, MN: Essential Library, 2016.

Don Nardo, *How Robotics Is Changing Society*. San Diego: ReferencePoint, 2015.

James Wolfe, ed., *Genetic Testing and Gene Therapy*. New York: Britannica Educational, 2015.

Websites

American Cancer Society (www.cancer.org). The American Cancer Society maintains up-to-date information about the latest precision medicine treatments available for each kind of cancer.

Qualcomm Tricorder XPRIZE (http://tricorder.xprize.org). The official website for the Tricorder XPRIZE competition keeps visitors informed about the final teams, their progress, and the latest news.

Robotics Trends (www.roboticstrends.com). At this site, visitors can keep up with all that is happening in the field of robotics. Click on the Health and Sports sections for the latest medical breakthroughs.

Wake Forest Institute for Regenerative Medicine: Wake Forest School of Medicine (www.wakehealth.edu/WFIRM). This is the official website of the institute that Anthony Atala directs. The photos and videos of the research team's work are fascinating and worth a look.

WT: Wearable Technologies (www.wearable-technologies. com). At this website, visitors can follow all the latest wearable news and learn about the latest inventions.

Index

Picture Credits

Cover: Depositphotos

6: Depositphotos

7: Depositphotos

10: Photofest Images

14: Tim Dominick/MCT/Newscom

17: Depositphotos

19: Joan Barnett Lee/Zuma Press/Newscom

25: Europics/Newscom

28: Mario Tama/Getty Images

32: BSIP/Newscom

35: Will & Deni McIntyre/Science Source

39: Jan Woitas/dpa/picture-alliance/Newscom

43: Du Cane Medical Imaging Ltd./Science Source

47: Sam Ogden/Science Source

50: Associated Press

54: AJ Photo/Science Source

58: David Chang/EPA/Newscom

62: Roberto A.Penne-Casanova/Science Source

64: Depositphotos

About the Author

Toney Allman holds degrees from Ohio State University and the University of Hawaii. She currently lives in Virginia, where she enjoys a rural lifestyle as well as researching and writing about a variety of topics for students.